KEEPING TIME

Praying Lent
Throughout the School Day

KEEPING TIME

Praying Lent
Throughout the School Day

Sandra Iwanski

saint mary's press

DEDICATION

To Jonathan, Christopher, and David,
who bless every season of my life . . .

The publishing team included Roxane Kadrlik Chlachula, development editor; Lorraine Kilmartin, reviewer; Image Farm/Picturequest, cover image; prepress and manufacturing coordinated by the production departments of Saint Mary's Press.

The scriptural quotations in this book are from the New American Bible with Revised New Testament and Revised Psalms. Copyright © 1991, 1986, and 1970 by the Confraternity of Christian Doctrine, Washington, D.C. Used by the permission of the copyright owner. All rights reserved. No part of the New American Bible may be reproduced in any form without permission in writing from the copyright owner.

The closing prayer for each day of Lent is from the song "A Dominican Blessing," by Sr. Mary Jean Traeger, based on a prayer by Blessed Jordan of Saxony. Copyright © 1983, 1997 by Sr. Mary Jean Traeger, OP, and the Springfield Dominican Sisters. All rights reserved. Used with permission of the author and the Springfield Dominican Sisters.

During this book's preparation, all citations, facts, figures, names, addresses, telephone numbers, Internet URLs, and other pieces of information cited within were verified for accuracy. The authors and Saint Mary's Press staff have made every attempt to reference current and valid sources, but we cannot guarantee the content of any source, and we are not responsible for any changes that may have occurred since our verification. If you find an error in, or have a question or concern about, any of the information or sources listed within, please contact Saint Mary's Press.

Copyright © 2009 by Sandra Iwanski. All rights reserved. No part of this book may be reproduced by any means without the written permission of the publisher, Saint Mary's Press, Christian Brothers Publications, 702 Terrace Heights, Winona, MN 55987-1320, www.smp.org.

Printed in the United States of America

3834

ISBN 978-0-88489-756-9, Print
ISBN 978-1-59982-201-3, Digital

CONTENTS

Introduction 7

Ash Wednesday 8

First Week of Lent 15

Second Week of Lent 27

Third Week of Lent 39

Fourth Week of Lent 51

Fifth Week of Lent 63

Sixth Week of Lent 75

INTRODUCTION

There is a rhythm to life. The Genesis promise of breathing in and breathing out is brought to life in the way our Church celebrates the seasons of the year . . . and in the way we move through our days.

As a Catholic high school, we invite our school community to walk in a prayerful rhythm. The natural cadence of our day includes all the bells and classes and adjusted schedules of any high school; however, we also build in moments of pause, moments of prayer, moments to notice the breathing in and breathing out of God's Spirit.

This book offers young people a way to observe a Lenten pause at the beginning of every class. As we journey through Lent, we realize that our prayer, fasting, and acts of charity prepare us to receive the salvation of Christ. These prayers are offered as a way for young people to honor the rhythms of the day and of the season.

The format reflects a tempo that is familiar to us. The leader (teacher or student) begins with the sign of the cross:

We begin this class as we begin all things:
In the name of the Father
and of the Son
and of the Holy Spirit. Amen.

Each day of Lent begins with a passage from the Scriptures. The rhythm of repeating the passage throughout the day helps us remember it. A short prayer follows the Scripture passage. After reading the prayer, the leader may choose to move to the final blessing, include a prayer everyone knows by heart, or invite particular intentions from the class. The following blessing comes from the Dominican tradition and is rooted in the writings of Blessed Jordan of Saxony, later adapted by Sr. Mary Jean Traeger, OP, a Springfield Dominican. You may choose to end your prayer time with this blessing or with one that is unique to your school or order:

May God, Creator, bless us
May God, Redeemer, heal us
May the Holy Spirit enlighten us
and give us all we need.

(Traeger, "A Dominican Blessing")

ASH WEDNESDAY

Opening Prayer

We begin this class as we begin all things:
**In the name of the Father
and of the Son
and of the Holy Spirit. Amen.**

Scripture Reading

Working together, then, we appeal to you not to receive the grace of God in vain. For he says:
"In an acceptable time I heard you,
and on the day of salvation I helped you."
Behold, now is a very acceptable time; behold, now is the day of salvation.

2 Corinthians 6:1–2

First Hour

God of all times and places, our Lent begins. Whether or not it feels like Lent to us, these forty days serve a purpose: by walking through these days with you, we prepare our hearts for the Lenten days that will come to each of us in some season of our lives. "Now is a very acceptable time; behold, now is the day of salvation."

Second Hour

God of all times and places, ashes mark our foreheads; in a smudged sign of the cross, we are public Christians. We hope these forty days will help us to be ready for the times when we will struggle in our prayer. "Now is a very acceptable time; behold, now is the day of salvation."

Third Hour

God of all times and places, the rhythm of Lent assumes that we are fasting from something that matters. Today we decide what we can eliminate from every day that will move us a step closer to being more like you. "Now is a very acceptable time; behold, now is the day of salvation."

Fourth Hour

God of all times and places, help us to keep our promise to pray, to honor the fast we have chosen, to share what we have with those who need it, to forgive and ask forgiveness, and to consider the part that suffering plays in our lives. "Now is a very acceptable time; behold, now is the day of salvation."

Fifth Hour

God of all times and places, when you see us, you see the deepest parts of us—the parts you made to be good and holy. Help us to see those deepest parts. "Now is a very acceptable time; behold, now is the day of salvation."

Sixth Hour

God of all times and places, it is time to notice that you are here in this moment. Bless us as we try to discover you and be patient as we struggle to find you. "Now is a very acceptable time; behold, now is the day of salvation."

Seventh Hour

God of all times and places, all around the world, people are making Lenten promises. We will not say our promises out loud. We pray that our Lenten lives will tell the story of what we promise you today. "Now is a very acceptable time; behold, now is the day of salvation."

Eighth Hour

God of all times and places, as the school day comes to a close, we thank you for this season. Thank you for the chance to admit to each other that sometimes life is hard . . . and to know that life was hard for you too. "Now is a very acceptable time; behold, now is the day of salvation."

Closing Blessing

We sign ourselves with the sign of our faith as we pray:

May God, Creator, bless us
May God, Redeemer, heal us
May the Holy Spirit enlighten us
and give us all we need.

THURSDAY

following Ash Wednesday

Opening Prayer

We begin this class as we begin all things:
**In the name of the Father
and of the Son
and of the Holy Spirit. Amen.**

Scripture Reading

Then he said to all, "If anyone wishes to come after me, he must deny himself and take up his cross daily and follow me. . . . What profit is there for one to gain the whole world yet lose or forfeit himself?"

Luke 9:23–25

First Hour

God of questions and answers, sometimes we don't feel close to you . . . we don't feel close to anyone. Sometimes we are in the middle of a terrible, very bad, no-good day. Is that what a cross is like? We wonder: can we actually follow you?

Second Hour

God of questions and answers, during Lent help us to face the tough questions about what it means to follow you. Lead us to the answer. We wonder: can we actually follow you?

Third Hour

God of questions and answers, if the invitation is to take up our cross and follow, then we need to move from where we are to another way of thinking, another way of being in this school. We wonder: can we actually follow you?

Fourth Hour

God of questions and answers, our "free will" can be a terrible and wonderful gift. We can freely will to follow you, to confront our own crosses—or not. We wonder: can we actually follow you?

Fifth Hour

God of questions and answers, we would be less than honest if we did not admit that most of the time, we do everything we can to avoid suffering, sadness—anything that is painful or difficult. Is there something to be learned from the cross? We wonder: can we actually follow you?

Sixth Hour

God of questions and answers, it sounds like you expect every human being to have a cross to bear. This Lent help us to confront our personal crosses. Help us to be honest about the struggles and to somehow learn from them. We wonder: can we actually follow you?

Seventh Hour

God of questions and answers, in our most honest moments, we admit that we want to run away from the cross. You loved your Apostles, and yet you told them they needed to struggle with the hard stuff. We wonder: can we actually follow you?

Eighth Hour

God of questions and answers, our crosses are unique. Help us this Lent to face the challenges that make each of our lives exceptional. We wonder: can we actually follow you?

Closing Blessing

We sign ourselves with the sign of our faith as we pray:

May God, Creator, bless us
May God, Redeemer, heal us
May the Holy Spirit enlighten us
and give us all we need.

FRIDAY
following Ash Wednesday

Opening Prayer

We begin this class as we begin all things:
**In the name of the Father
and of the Son
and of the Holy Spirit. Amen.**

Scripture Reading

*This, rather, is the fasting that I wish:
releasing those bound unjustly,
untying the thongs of the yoke;
Setting free the oppressed,
breaking every yoke;
Sharing your bread with the hungry,
sheltering the oppressed and the homeless. . . .
Then your light shall break forth like the dawn.*

Isaiah 58:6–8

First Hour

God in our real lives, today we will walk past people who are unjustly bound to the label others have given them—the label some of us in this room have given them. If we can admit they are children of God, that gift can set them free. It is Lent: let your light break forth in us like the dawn.

Second Hour

God in our real lives, what does it look like to walk through a school day and be oppressed—to not be free to let people know who we really are? We can sacrifice our judgments and give the gift of your truth. It is Lent: let your light break forth in us like the dawn.

Third Hour

God in our real lives, most of us had breakfast today, and it is hard for us to imagine what it is like to be hungry. What alms can we give that would feed someone who is hungry? It is Lent: let your light break forth in us like the dawn.

Fourth Hour

God in our real lives, does everyone feel "at home" in our school? Could it be that homelessness is not only about having a roof over our heads? Today, teach us how we can make everyone feel at home in our classrooms . . . in the cafeteria . . . in the locker room . . . in the gym. It is Lent: let your light break forth in us like the dawn.

Fifth Hour

God in our real lives, there is someone who wouldn't feel tied up in knots if he or she heard a word of encouragement from us. Perhaps that is the fast you want: to put aside whatever keeps us from appreciating and encouraging others. It is Lent: let your light break forth in us like the dawn.

Sixth Hour

God in our real lives, it is time to ask ourselves what goes through our minds when we hear someone talk about those who are homeless. Do we assume they are simply not doing anything about their situation, or do we ask what part we play in making sure everyone has a safe home? It is Lent: let your light break forth in us like the dawn.

Seventh Hour

God in our real lives, it seems like you are telling us that there is some connection between a religious practice like Lenten fasting and justice. Help us to understand so that we can bring justice to our school. It is Lent: let your light break forth in us like the dawn.

Eighth Hour

God in our real lives, this Lent help us to do more than just go through the motions. We can talk about prayer, fasting, and acts of charity—this time teach us how to live prayer, fasting, and acts of charity. It is Lent: let your light break forth in us like the dawn.

Closing Blessing

We sign ourselves with the sign of our faith as we pray:
    May God, Creator, bless us
    May God, Redeemer, heal us
    May the Holy Spirit enlighten us
    and give us all we need.

Shutterstock

FIRST
WEEK OF LENT

MONDAY

First Week of Lent

Opening Prayer

We begin this class as we begin all things:
**In the name of the Father
and of the Son
and of the Holy Spirit. Amen.**

Scripture Reading

"And he will separate them one from another. . . . Then the king will say to those on his right, . . . 'Inherit the kingdom prepared for you from the foundation of the world. For I was hungry . . . I was thirsty . . . a stranger . . . naked . . . ill . . . in prison.' . . . 'Amen, I say to you, whatever you did for one of these least brothers of mine, you did for me.'"

Matthew 25:32–40

First Hour

God living among us, help us to see you. Help us to imagine the faces of students just like us who are trying to learn in the middle of chaos, and let our prayers encircle them with your love. Can we really be seeing you in those who suffer?

Second Hour

God living among us, help us to see you. There are people we know who have burdens that are just too much for them to carry alone. Can we really be seeing you in those who suffer?

Third Hour

God living among us, we expect to see you in extraordinarily beautiful moments . . . in the faces of people who love one another . . . in perfect blue-sky days. You tell us to look for you in the faces of those who struggle . . . in the lives of those who are in pain. Can we really be seeing you in those who suffer?

Fourth Hour

God living among us, it can be a challenge to put it all together: to listen to what you have to say, and to wrestle with what we think we know about Lent and prayer. Can we really be seeing you in those who suffer?

Fifth Hour

God living among us, we are unsure about what you want us to do. What do you look like today? Help us to see who is in need and to make a difference somehow—perhaps just a small difference, but a step in the right direction. Can we really be seeing you in those who suffer?

Sixth Hour

God living among us, may we realize that you are not so far away. Help us to recognize you in the people who are close to us—moms and dads, brothers and sisters, teachers and coaches, principals and deans, friends and neighbors. Teach us to honor those who are closest to us. Can we really be seeing you in those who suffer?

Seventh Hour

God living among us, help us to see you. As we move through our busy day, help us to recognize the person who needs a word of encouragement or an act of kindness. Walk with us this Lent. Can we really be seeing you in those who suffer?

Eighth Hour

God living among us, sometimes it seems like a person has to be "the greatest" in order to matter at school. You do something different: you take care of the least as well as the greatest. Help us to act as you would act this Lent. Can we really be seeing you in those who suffer?

Closing Blessing

We sign ourselves with the sign of our faith as we pray:
> May God, Creator, bless us
> May God, Redeemer, heal us
> May the Holy Spirit enlighten us
> and give us all we need.

TUESDAY

First Week of Lent

Opening Prayer

We begin this class as we begin all things:
**In the name of the Father
and of the Son
and of the Holy Spirit. Amen.**

Scripture Reading

"When you fast, do not look gloomy like the hypocrites. They neglect their appearance, so that they may appear to others to be fasting. . . . When you fast, anoint your head and wash your face, so that you may not appear to others to be fasting, except to your Father who is hidden."

Matthew 6:16–18

First Hour

Hidden God, we have known people who loved you deeply. We call them to mind now and remember what they looked like [pause]. Help us to live like people who love you.

Second Hour

Hidden God, we remember the first person who taught us how to fold our hands . . . how to make the sign of the cross . . . how to say a prayer. Help us to live like people who love you.

Third Hour

Hidden God, when you lived among us, people just wanted to be close to you. They wondered what was different about you, what you knew that they did not know. Help us to live like people who love you.

Fourth Hour

Hidden God, if prayer, fasting, and acts of charity do not make us more loving and generous, then our Lenten practices will not lead people to ask what is different about our lives. Help us to live like people who love you.

Fifth Hour

Hidden God, these long days of Lent can teach us that change takes time. May our hearts experience conversion through our prayer, fasting, and works of charity. Help us to live like people who love you.

Sixth Hour

Hidden God, when someone passes us in the hall, when a parent asks how our day has been, as we move through our ordinary day, we count on our Lenten practices of prayer, fasting, and works of charity to remind us of your presence in our daily lives. Help us to live like people who love you.

Seventh Hour

Hidden God, we are beginning to sense that practicing Lent helps us remember that you are part of all we do. Help us to live like people who love you.

Eighth Hour

Hidden God, we have entered into Lenten fasting with the hope that in some mysterious way, our fasting will help us to be holy, to become whole, and to be whom you had in mind when you created us. Help us to live like people who love you.

Closing Blessing

We sign ourselves with the sign of our faith as we pray:
> May God, Creator, bless us
> May God, Redeemer, heal us
> May the Holy Spirit enlighten us
> and give us all we need.

WEDNESDAY

First Week of Lent

Opening Prayer

We begin this class as we begin all things:

**In the name of the Father
and of the Son
and of the Holy Spirit. Amen.**

Scripture Reading

*For just as from the heavens
  the rain and snow come down
And do not return there
  till they have watered the earth,
  making it fertile and fruitful,
Giving seed to him who sows
  and bread to him who eats,
So shall my word be
  that goes forth from my mouth;
It shall not return to me void,
  but shall do my will,
  achieving the end for which I sent it.*

Isaiah 55:10–11

First Hour

Patient God, we begin each prayer by listening to your Word in the Holy Scriptures. You assure us that somehow the Word in us will make a difference in the world. Don't give up . . . wait for us. Help us to be your Word today.

Second Hour

Patient God, you promise that your Word always bears fruit. Are you saying that when we hear your Word, something in our world will be different, someone in our world will know more love . . . more peace . . . more hope? Don't give up . . . wait for us. Help us to be your Word today.

Third Hour

Patient God, just like a gardener places a seed in the ground trusting that with sun and water and time a harvest will appear, you believe that when we hear your Word, it is planted inside of us and in time we will grow into your Kingdom. Don't give up . . . wait for us. Help us to be your Word today.

Fourth Hour

Patient God, your Word challenges us to grow—and sometimes growing means changing. This Lent is the time to be bold enough to change if that is what we need to do. Don't give up . . . wait for us. Help us to be your Word today.

Fifth Hour

Patient God, help us to hear your Word, so that how we live our lives can make a difference in the world. Don't give up . . . wait for us. Help us to be your Word today.

Sixth Hour

Patient God, your Word is life giving; may our words be life giving too. Slow us down enough to think before we speak today. Don't give up . . . wait for us. Help us to be your Word today.

Seventh Hour

Patient God, what if we are quieter than usual today? If your Word is planted in us, then how we live—not just what we say—will be apparent to those around us. Don't give up . . . wait for us. Help us to be your Word today.

Eighth Hour

Patient God, today's reading from Isaiah sounds like a promise: if we pay attention to your Word, the world will be different. We wonder what it would be like in our school if each of us spent three minutes a day thinking about the day's Scripture verse. Don't give up . . . wait for us. Help us to be your Word today.

Closing Blessing

We sign ourselves with the sign of our faith as we pray:
> **May God, Creator, bless us**
> **May God, Redeemer, heal us**
> **May the Holy Spirit enlighten us**
> **and give us all we need.**

THURSDAY

First Week of Lent

Opening Prayer

We begin this class as we begin all things:
**In the name of the Father
and of the Son
and of the Holy Spirit. Amen.**

Scripture Reading

*But if the wicked man turns away from all the sins he
committed, if he keeps all my statutes and does what is right
and just, he shall surely live. . . . He shall live because of
the virtue he has practiced.*

Ezekiel 18:21–22

First Hour

Source of all that is good and holy, you are willing to wipe the
slate clean . . . to turn back the clock . . . to press "delete."
Help us to turn away from what we know is wrong so that we may
experience your mercy and forgiveness. May we turn away from sin
and be faithful to the gospel.

Second Hour

Source of all that is good and holy, for some of us, there is a person
we are finding it very hard to forgive. We don't want to put the
past behind us and forgive. God, why is forgiveness sometimes so
difficult for us? May we turn away from sin and be faithful to the
gospel.

Third Hour

Source of all that is good and holy, when we are sorry, you are
willing to forgive and forget. If we follow you, we must also be
ready to forgive and forget. Help us to be more like you. May we
turn away from sin and be faithful to the gospel.

Fourth Hour

Source of all that is good and holy, you encourage us to take the first step and turn in another direction. In your goodness you offer us another choice: to turn away from what is "wicked" and toward what is "right and just." May we turn away from sin and be faithful to the gospel.

Fifth Hour

Source of all that is good and holy, before we can say we follow you, we must go to the people who have experienced our lapses into sin and ask for their forgiveness. It seems like it is easier to ask you for forgiveness than to face someone we have hurt. May we turn away from sin and be faithful to the gospel.

Sixth Hour

Source of all that is good and holy, we are thinking more than usual about the effects of our choices. Help us to practice virtue this Lent, because you tell us that will lead us to eternal life. May we turn away from sin and be faithful to the gospel.

Seventh Hour

Source of all that is good and holy, it is clear that you want us to choose virtue, to choose justice. It helps to know that you believe we can bring justice to this world. May we turn away from sin and be faithful to the gospel.

Eighth Hour

Source of all that is good and holy, don't let us move through these days as if we have all the time in the world. We have this life—not a moment more—to choose what is right. May we turn away from sin and be faithful to the gospel.

Closing Blessing

We sign ourselves with the sign of our faith as we pray:

> **May God, Creator, bless us**
> **May God, Redeemer, heal us**
> **May the Holy Spirit enlighten us**
> **and give us all we need.**

FRIDAY

First Week of Lent

Opening Prayer

We begin this class as we begin all things:
**In the name of the Father
and of the Son
and of the Holy Spirit. Amen.**

Scripture Reading

*"Come," they said, "let us contrive a plot against Jeremiah.
. . . And so, let us destroy him by his own tongue; let us
carefully note his every word." . . .*

> *Heed me, O LORD,
> and listen to what my adversaries say.
> Must good be repaid with evil . . . ?*

Jeremiah 18:18–20

First Hour

God with us, listen to the words we use today. What will it cost if
what we say out loud makes it clear that we are trying to follow
you? Can we be prophets in our school?

Second Hour

God with us, listen to the words we use today. Listen to how we
describe our classmates . . . how we talk about our teachers
. . . what we have to say about our families. Which side are we
on—Jeremiah's or his enemies'? Can we be prophets in our school?

Third Hour

God with us, listen to the words we use today. There will be
a day—maybe today or tomorrow or a week from now—when
someone will try to hurt us with words. Even when we are met
with evil, help us to hold on. Can we be prophets in our school?

Fourth Hour

God with us, listen to the words we use today. Do our words sound like something you would say? Jeremiah's enemies gave in to the temptation to hurt him with words. We ask that you help us resist the temptation to fight back with cruel words. Can we be prophets in our school?

Fifth Hour

God with us, listen to the words we use today. Help us to figure out the difference between the words that strengthen us and the words that destroy us. You know our weaknesses, so we count on you to be with us. Can we be prophets in our school?

Sixth Hour

God with us, listen to the words we use today. We choose to pay attention to how we name people. If we realized that the words we use to describe people are labels that are permanently attached to someone, we might think twice about how we use our words. Can we be prophets in our school?

Seventh Hour

God with us, listen to the words we use today. What message do we want the world to hear? Do we really believe that your love can change this world? Our school will hear a message about you today. It will be shared in what we say and how we treat each other. Can we be prophets in our school?

Eighth Hour

God with us, listen to the words we use today. Help us to confront the truth: sometimes our lives are ordinary, and yet you are always mysteriously present to us—even in the ordinary. Help us to hear your mystery echo when we speak to each other. Can we be prophets in our school?

Closing Blessing

We sign ourselves with the sign of our faith as we pray:

> **May God, Creator, bless us**
> **May God, Redeemer, heal us**
> **May the Holy Spirit enlighten us**
> **and give us all we need.**

Shutterstock

SECOND
WEEK OF LENT

MONDAY

Second Week of Lent

Opening Prayer

We begin this class as we begin all things:
**In the name of the Father
and of the Son
and of the Holy Spirit. Amen.**

Scripture Reading

"Ask and it will be given to you; seek and you will find; knock and the door will be opened to you. For everyone who asks, receives; and the one who seeks, finds; and to the one who knocks, the door will be opened."

Matthew 7:7–8

First Hour

We speak your name, and you hear our prayer. First there was you—our Creator God, and now there is us—God's creation. We ask that our lives be a reflection of you. We take you at your Word: "Ask and it will be given to you."

Second Hour

We speak your name, and you hear our prayer. We know that you are present in every one of us. We ask that we are able to honor your presence in the person we find it hardest to love. We take you at your Word: "Ask and it will be given to you."

Third Hour

We speak your name, and you hear our prayer. We ask that we will have the courage, commitment, and fortitude to continue our Lenten practices of praying, fasting, and acts of charity. We take you at your Word: "Ask and it will be given to you."

Fourth Hour

We speak your name, and you hear our prayer. Lent sets aside time for thinking, action, and conversion. We ask that our days in this school empower each one of us to become everything you imagine us to be. We take you at your Word: "Ask and it will be given to you."

Fifth Hour

We speak your name, and you hear our prayer. We are part of a faith tradition that dreams of a world of justice and peace. We ask for the grace to be transformed this Lent so that we may discover what is good and perfect. We take you at your Word: "Ask and it will be given to you."

Sixth Hour

We speak your name, and you hear our prayer. We ask you to help us remember that words about you are not you—they are simply words. We take you at your Word: "Ask and it will be given to you."

Seventh Hour

We speak your name, and you hear our prayer. We are doing our best to find you this Lent. It can be tempting to turn away because we are struggling with questions about who you are and what you have planned for us. We take you at your Word: "Ask and it will be given to you."

Eighth Hour

We speak your name, and you hear our prayer. We need to know that other people in this school are searching for you too. We ask for the courage to continue the journey and for companions along the way. We take you at your Word: "Ask and it will be given to you."

Closing Blessing

We sign ourselves with the sign of our faith as we pray:
> **May God, Creator, bless us**
> **May God, Redeemer, heal us**
> **May the Holy Spirit enlighten us**
> **and give us all we need.**

TUESDAY

Second Week of Lent

Opening Prayer

We begin this class as we begin all things:
**In the name of the Father
and of the Son
and of the Holy Spirit. Amen.**

Scripture Reading

*"Stop judging, that you may not be judged. For as you
judge, so will you be judged, and the measure with which
you measure will be measured out to you."*

Matthew 7:1–2

First Hour

God of possibilities, this can become a place where people are
treated in an extraordinary way, where kind words transform
lives, where truth lives. May the love we measure out to others be
measured out to us.

Second Hour

God of possibilities, using your eyes we can look at our companions
in this place and judge them to be holy: singularly unique,
particularly loved, and set apart by you. May the love we measure
out to others be measured out to us.

Third Hour

God of possibilities, help us to welcome the strangers among us.
Help us to welcome the people who live in a different neighborhood
and those who choose different friends or go to another school.
May the love we measure out to others be measured out to us.

Fourth Hour

God of possibilities, admitting to ourselves that you know our most
secret thoughts, we consider the judgments we make of others in

the recesses of our minds—the judgments of others that we never speak out loud but hold in the quiet of our hearts. May the love we measure out to others be measured out to us.

Fifth Hour

God of possibilities, this Lent we are beginning to confront the truth that we always get to choose—we get to choose whether our words are life giving or hurtful. Help us pay attention to our words of judgment today. May the love we measure out to others be measured out to us.

Sixth Hour

God of possibilities, some of us struggle with your lesson on judging others; it is tempting to listen to mean-spirited talk and to say "everyone does it." We know that is not true, and we count on you to help us turn things around. May the love we measure out to others be measured out to us.

Seventh Hour

God of possibilities, it is possible that you have a plan for our lives and for the lives of the people we care about. We pray for the grace and courage to release the people we love into your hands—not judging the plan, but trusting the plan. May the love we measure out to others be measured out to us.

Eighth Hour

God of possibilities, people all over the world will live today in poverty, in the midst of violence, under the shadow of oppression. Give us the courage to speak up for fair wages, peaceful homes, and just societies. May the love we measure out to others be measured out to us.

Closing Blessing

We sign ourselves with the sign of our faith as we pray:
> **May God, Creator, bless us**
> **May God, Redeemer, heal us**
> **May the Holy Spirit enlighten us**
> **and give us all we need.**

WEDNESDAY

Second Week of Lent

Opening Prayer

We begin this class as we begin all things:
In the name of the Father
and of the Son
and of the Holy Spirit. Amen.

Scripture Reading

"Which is the first of all the commandments?" Jesus replied, "The first is this: . . . 'You shall love the Lord your God with all your heart, with all your soul, with all your mind, and with all your strength.' The second is this: 'You shall love your neighbor as yourself.'"

Mark 12:28–31

First Hour

God of love, our families are woven together with the stories and practices of many religious traditions. Here in this school may we be an example of living in harmony and respecting what is different and unique in how we approach you. On this Lenten day, we will love our neighbors as ourselves.

Second Hour

God of love, let us honor the questions and stories that fill our lives and pray that debate, dialogue, and reform will build up the communion of saints living among us. On this Lenten day, we will love our neighbors as ourselves.

Third Hour

God of love, empower the leaders of our school so that through their example we will deepen the respect we have for all who love God. On this Lenten day, we will love our neighbors as ourselves.

Fourth Hour

God of love, your invitation to live this great commandment is given to everyone: the rich, the poor, the leaders, the followers, the unemployed, the homeless, the friend, and the enemy. On this Lenten day, we will love our neighbors as ourselves.

Fifth Hour

God of love, we wonder, why is it so easy to point to the faults of others when it is so hard to hear our own shortcomings spoken out loud? Teach us about love. On this Lenten day, we will love our neighbors as ourselves.

Sixth Hour

God of love, we call to mind now the person in this community we find it hardest to love: the person who annoys us, irritates us, and drives us crazy. As we picture that person, we hear your voice again. On this Lenten day, we will love our neighbors as ourselves.

Seventh Hour

God of love, it takes courage to speak against those who use their power to exploit others—in the classroom, in our families, in our friendships. We are all neighbors. On this Lenten day, we will love our neighbors as ourselves.

Eighth Hour

God of love, loving everyone is so big. We have to believe that every little bit counts and that somehow you will put it all together into a Kingdom that loves. On this Lenten day, we will love our neighbors as ourselves.

Closing Blessing

We sign ourselves with the sign of our faith as we pray:
> **May God, Creator, bless us**
> **May God, Redeemer, heal us**
> **May the Holy Spirit enlighten us**
> **and give us all we need.**

THURSDAY

Second Week of Lent

Opening Prayer

We begin this class as we begin all things:
**In the name of the Father
and of the Son
and of the Holy Spirit. Amen.**

Scripture Reading

"Listen to my voice; then I will be your God and you shall be my people. Walk in all the ways that I command you, so that you may prosper."

Jeremiah 7:23–24

First Hour

Ever-present God, our lives get all tangled up, and some days it is hard to hear your voice. Every day we decide whether or not to listen to what you have to say: "Listen to my voice; then I will be your God and you shall be my people."

Second Hour

Ever-present God, if we listen, is it possible that our lives will be so like yours that no one will be able to tell where your life ends and ours begin? "Listen to my voice; then I will be your God and you shall be my people."

Third Hour

Ever-present God, there are people in my life that I refuse to pay attention to when they speak to me. Forgive me for the times I would not listen to you and the people you have put in my life. "Listen to my voice; then I will be your God and you shall be my people."

Fourth Hour

Ever-present God, when we listen carefully to what you dream for us to be, it will be clear to others that we are letting you into our lives. "Listen to my voice; then I will be your God and you shall be my people."

Fifth Hour

Ever-present God, we are learning that life is often a struggle between good and evil. We pray for the courage to take a stand for what is good—and that we will take responsibility for being part of what divides us. "Listen to my voice; then I will be your God and you shall be my people."

Sixth Hour

Ever-present God, we say that distractions keep us from listening for your voice: too much schoolwork, chores to do at home, jobs, friends . . . Forgive us for being slaves to whatever keeps us from letting you into our lives. "Listen to my voice; then I will be your God and you shall be my people."

Seventh Hour

Ever-present God, could it be an unforgiving spirit that keeps us from listening to you? Forgive us for the times we have refused to forgive, and lead us to open our heart to the person who has hurt us. "Listen to my voice; then I will be your God and you shall be my people."

Eighth Hour

Ever-present God, some of us have kept you captive in our theology books. We have not listened for your voice, but instead listened for the answers to the questions on the next test. We pray that we can release you from our textbooks and let you into our lives. "Listen to my voice; then I will be your God and you shall be my people."

Closing Blessing

We sign ourselves with the sign of our faith as we pray:

May God, Creator, bless us
May God, Redeemer, heal us
May the Holy Spirit enlighten us
and give us all we need.

FRIDAY

Second Week of Lent

Opening Prayer

We begin this class as we begin all things:
**In the name of the Father
and of the Son
and of the Holy Spirit. Amen.**

Scripture Reading

When Mary [the sister of Lazarus] came to where Jesus was and saw him, she fell at his feet and said to him, "Lord, if you had been here, my brother would not have died." When Jesus saw her weeping and the Jews who had come with her weeping, he became perturbed and deeply troubled, and said, "Where have you laid him?" They said to him, "Sir, come and see." And Jesus wept. So the Jews said, "See how he loved him."

John 11:32–36

First Hour

God who cries with friends, there are men and women and children whose eyes search every crowd for hints of a suicide bomber. And Jesus wept.

Second Hour

God who cries with friends, there are parents who spent the night at the bedside of a gravely ill child, and you sat with them. And Jesus wept.

Third Hour

God who cries with friends, people we love are battling devastating illnesses, and we try everything we can think of to somehow make these days easier for them. And Jesus wept.

Fourth Hour

God who cries with friends, there are men and women and children all over the world who wonder what they will eat today—some of them are nearby . . . some of them are us. If we share, there is enough for everyone. So why are some people hungry? And Jesus wept.

Fifth Hour

God who cries with friends, we wish you could explain to us why the world suffers unimaginable disasters like hurricanes, earthquakes, and floods. We see the pictures and hear the news and collect food, clothing, and toys for those in need. It doesn't make sense that lives are reshaped by natural disasters. And Jesus wept.

Sixth Hour

God who cries with friends, addiction is like a stranglehold on a life . . . like being captured . . . like being deaf to the voice of God reminding us that we are beloved. Some of us know addiction too well. Addiction ensnares us or someone we love, and we cry out in the night. And Jesus wept.

Seventh Hour

God who cries with friends, you know what we fear the most. When we are afraid, we know we are not alone. You promised to walk through the dark places in our lives with us, and it helps to have someone right there. And Jesus wept.

Eighth Hour

God who cries with friends, you understand that it is not just the big things that get us down, that bring us to tears. And so we ask you to be present as we work to be free of everything that holds us down today . . . everything that keeps us from having the day you imagined for us when we were created. And Jesus wept.

Closing Blessing

We sign ourselves with the sign of our faith as we pray:

> **May God, Creator, bless us**
> **May God, Redeemer, heal us**
> **May the Holy Spirit enlighten us**
> **and give us all we need.**

Shutterstock

THIRD
WEEK OF LENT

MONDAY

Third Week of Lent

Opening Prayer

We begin this class as we begin all things:
**In the name of the Father
and of the Son
and of the Holy Spirit. Amen.**

Scripture Reading

*Blessed is the man who trusts in the LORD,
whose hope is the LORD.*

Jeremiah 17:7

First Hour

Trustworthy One, you have placed us in this school on purpose. We are in a place that always looks to you first, anticipates our holiness, and reminds us that we are beloved. Our hope is in the Lord.

Second Hour

Trustworthy One, the season of Lent is here. We pray that our sacrifices of prayer, fasting, and acts of charity will empower us to recognize you in our lives. Our hope is in the Lord.

Third Hour

Trustworthy One, your Word is filled with promises of what we can hope for: peace, charity, justice, patience, joy, wholeness, service. We long for a world where all your promises come true. Our hope is in the Lord.

Fourth Hour

Trustworthy One, you believe that we can change the world. You believe that one by one we can bring a peace that is beyond all understanding to each person who stands beside us. We hope that all things are really possible with God. Our hope is in the Lord.

Fifth Hour

Trustworthy One, if we are thinking Lenten thoughts, then it is clear that you are no longer a baby in Bethlehem. You have grown in wisdom, age, and grace, and have found your voice. You are moving closer to the cross, and we are moving closer to understanding that you speak to us and through us. Our hope is in the Lord.

Sixth Hour

Trustworthy One, this is it. We won't get the chance to live this Lenten day again. Turn our attention to the details of our lives: we are part of an incredible story woven by the people who love us. It is a story we help you to write. Our hope is in the Lord.

Seventh Hour

Trustworthy One, Christian churches everywhere depend on Lent to remind us that we can live like a saint: unique, beloved, whole, unhurried, and unafraid. On a busy Lenten school day, we hold on to the promise that really living this season can help us to be more like you. Our hope is in the Lord.

Eighth Hour

Trustworthy One, we want to know what is right. It is not just the right answer we want; we want the right way of being, of dating, of speaking, of studying, of working, of loving. We are counting on you to speak to our hearts—or maybe to our conscience—so that we know how to choose. Our hope is in the Lord.

Closing Blessing

We sign ourselves with the sign of our faith as we pray:
> **May God, Creator, bless us**
> **May God, Redeemer, heal us**
> **May the Holy Spirit enlighten us**
> **and give us all we need.**

TUESDAY
Third Week of Lent

Opening Prayer

We begin this class as we begin all things:
**In the name of the Father
and of the Son
and of the Holy Spirit. Amen.**

Scripture Reading

He went down with them and came to Nazareth, and was obedient to them. . . . And Jesus advanced [in] wisdom and age and favor before God and man.

Luke 2:51–52

First Hour

Son of God, it is easy to forget that you were once the age of the students who fill this school. Your example reminds us that we have people in our lives who will help us on our way. Together may we grow in wisdom, age, and grace.

Second Hour

Son of God, sometimes it feels like our lives are filled with rules. There are codes of conduct and curfews, computer guidelines and rules of the road, house rules and church rules. You are the Son of God, and even you obeyed. Together may we grow in wisdom, age, and grace.

Third Hour

Son of God, what would happen if we filled this place with good works, if we thought good thoughts, if we spoke only good words? Together may we grow in wisdom, age, and grace.

Fourth Hour

Son of God, we admit that we allow some of your children to move through our classrooms unnoticed. Your wisdom leads us to open our hearts and lives wide enough to let in everyone. Together may we grow in wisdom, age, and grace.

Fifth Hour

Son of God, remembering that you were once our age helps us realize that you too had parents in your life. Our mothers and fathers are not perfect, they are simply human—they worry, they struggle, they dream. Together may we grow in wisdom, age, and grace.

Sixth Hour

Son of God, there are people in this building who encourage us to become everything we can be. This Lent, lead us to a spirit of gratitude for the ones in our lives who point us in the right direction. Together may we grow in wisdom, age, and grace.

Seventh Hour

Son of God, thinking about the business of your Father in the Temple reminds us that you were always God—both God and man. "Both-and" is the critical part, the confusing part—the faith part. Together may we grow in wisdom, age, and grace.

Eighth Hour

Son of God, we cannot lock you safely away in our Bible stories. It looks like you have something to do with every part of us—including the son and daughter parts of us. Together may we grow in wisdom, age, and grace.

Closing Blessing

We sign ourselves with the sign of our faith as we pray:
> **May God, Creator, bless us**
> **May God, Redeemer, heal us**
> **May the Holy Spirit enlighten us**
> **and give us all we need.**

WEDNESDAY

Third Week of Lent

Opening Prayer

We begin this class as we begin all things:
**In the name of the Father
and of the Son
and of the Holy Spirit. Amen.**

Scripture Reading

"But as for the seed that fell on rich soil, they are the ones who, when they have heard the word, embrace it with a generous and good heart, and bear fruit through perseverance."

Luke 8:15

First Hour

Persistent God, in the middle of this Lent we ask for the grace to say yes to all the possibilities: yes to the uncomfortable stretching it takes to become something new. May we bear fruit through perseverance.

Second Hour

Persistent God, goodness and generosity demand that we keep our eyes open. We need eyes to notice what is happening in our school today and grace to realize that in this place you are teaching us about life and about love. May we bear fruit through perseverance.

Third Hour

Persistent God, some people believe that war can't be helped, that it is just the way things are. You teach us that peace is more than a possibility, that peace is our destiny. We continue to seek peace in our lives. May we bear fruit through perseverance.

Fourth Hour

Persistent God, in our school we continue to talk about Lent . . . and think about Lent . . . and pray about Lent. Catholic schools have long been committed to the talking, thinking, and praying that will lead people to you. In our Catholic school, we continue to follow. May we bear fruit through perseverance.

Fifth Hour

Persistent God, what have you tried to plant in our hearts this Lent? We live in a world that seems to pay no attention to you, and we wonder if we are, in fact, good soil. We can help each other to hear you. May we bear fruit through perseverance.

Sixth Hour

Persistent God, if the lessons you have planted in our lives this Lent actually take root, then it is possible that the lives of the people in our school will be so like the life of Jesus that no one will be able to tell where Jesus's life ends and ours begins! Help us continue to help each other grow. May we bear fruit through perseverance.

Seventh Hour

Persistent God, you keep encouraging us to grow. As we notice the difference our Lenten prayer, fasting, and acts of charity are making in someone's life, we can give them the gift of noticing. May we bear fruit through perseverance.

Eighth Hour

Persistent God, the parables you shared are rooted in real life. Our challenge is to release our faith from stories and live it in real life. We continue to look for ways to tell your story in our lives. May we bear fruit through perseverance.

Closing Blessing

We sign ourselves with the sign of our faith as we pray:
> **May God, Creator, bless us**
> **May God, Redeemer, heal us**
> **May the Holy Spirit enlighten us**
> **and give us all we need.**

THURSDAY

Third Week of Lent

Opening Prayer

We begin this class as we begin all things:
**In the name of the Father
and of the Son
and of the Holy Spirit. Amen.**

Scripture Reading

"But to you who hear I say, love your enemies, do good to those who hate you, bless those who curse you, pray for those who mistreat you. . . . For if you love those who love you, what credit is that to you? Even sinners love those who love them. . . . Be merciful, just as your Father is merciful."

Luke 6:27–36

First Hour

Challenging God, as we get closer to Easter, we need to confront the truth about death and resurrection. When we die, you will want to talk about how we made a difference in the world and how we loved those around us. It's not always easy. "Even sinners love those who love them. . . . Be merciful, just as your Father is merciful."

Second Hour

Challenging God, it sounds like you are asking us to let go of every part of our lives that is ungodly. This talk about loving enemies is a struggle. "Even sinners love those who love them. . . . Be merciful, just as your Father is merciful."

Third Hour

Challenging God, Lent gives us time to take a long, hard look at our lives and ask whether we actually love you with all our heart, with all our soul, and with all our mind. "Even sinners love those who love them. . . . Be merciful, just as your Father is merciful."

Fourth Hour

Challenging God, so everyone is our neighbor? This Lent help us to have a new understanding of how we are all connected. You say that someone who follows you loves everyone. "Even sinners love those who love them. . . . Be merciful, just as your Father is merciful."

Fifth Hour

Challenging God, we admit it: Lent is hard work and loving is hard work. Encourage us—we've decided to do the hard work and dream your dream of a Kingdom. "Even sinners love those who love them. . . . Be merciful, just as your Father is merciful."

Sixth Hour

Challenging God, help us to realize that you are a part of our joys and successes as well as our challenges and disappointments. We accept your challenge to love, and we count on you staying with us. "Even sinners love those who love them. . . . Be merciful, just as your Father is merciful."

Seventh Hour

Challenging God, you are ready to embrace everyone—despite their good choices or bad choices. Today we hope for a world that will abandon the sorrow of life destroyed and turn to the joy of a new life. "Even sinners love those who love them. . . . Be merciful, just as your Father is merciful."

Eighth Hour

Challenging God, we call to mind all those in ministry. May their lives give strong witness to what it means to love every one of us. "Even sinners love those who love them. . . . Be merciful, just as your Father is merciful."

Closing Blessing

We sign ourselves with the sign of our faith as we pray:
> **May God, Creator, bless us**
> **May God, Redeemer, heal us**
> **May the Holy Spirit enlighten us**
> **and give us all we need.**

FRIDAY

Third Week of Lent

Opening Prayer

We begin this class as we begin all things:
In the name of the Father
and of the Son
and of the Holy Spirit. Amen.

Scripture Reading

Fear not, for I have redeemed you;
I have called you by name: you are mine. . . .
For I am the LORD, your God,
the Holy One of Israel, your savior.

Isaiah 43:1–3

First Hour

Holy One of Israel, today we consider the fearless ones who face a health crisis and continue to follow you. We pray for courage for the men and women who staff AIDS clinics. You have called them by name: they are yours.

Second Hour

Holy One of Israel, we pray for the dedicated women and men who staff crisis pregnancy centers and who save countless babies and countless moms and dads from the ravages of abortion. You have called them by name: they are yours.

Third Hour

Holy One of Israel, we pray for the men and women who staff homeless shelters—so that homeless men, women, and children will have a clean, safe place to stay for the night. You have called them by name: they are yours.

Fourth Hour

Holy One of Israel, we pray for the women and men who boldly speak out against war and who remind us that there must be another way—please, there must be another way. You have called them by name: they are yours.

Fifth Hour

Holy One of Israel, we pray for the women and men who staff soup kitchens so that those who are hungry and poor may have a hot meal. You have called them by name: they are yours.

Sixth Hour

Holy One of Israel, there are people we call missionaries—some who travel to far-off places to tell others about God and others who stay close to home—right here in our schools, in our families, and in our churches. All of them struggle to find the right time, the right place, the right words to introduce you to us. You have called them by name: they are yours.

Seventh Hour

Holy One of Israel, we worry about taking the right classes and getting the right grade . . . about building a close relationship with someone we care about . . . about families that aren't working right . . . about making it through the day and then making it through the night. You promised that you would be with us. You have called us by name: we are yours.

Eighth Hour

Holy One of Israel, it is the end of the day . . . and the end of the week. Walk with us through this weekend when we are tempted to forget that it is Lent or even to forget that we are yours. You have called us by name: we are yours.

Closing Blessing

We sign ourselves with the sign of our faith as we pray:
May God, Creator, bless us
May God, Redeemer, heal us
May the Holy Spirit enlighten us
and give us all we need.

Shutterstock

FOURTH
WEEK OF LENT

MONDAY

Fourth Week of Lent

Opening Prayer

We begin this class as we begin all things:
**In the name of the Father
and of the Son
and of the Holy Spirit. Amen.**

Scripture Reading

"Two people went up to the temple area to pray; one was a Pharisee and the other was a tax collector. The Pharisee took up his position and spoke this prayer to himself, 'O God, I thank you that I am not like the rest of humanity . . . or even like this tax collector. . . . But the tax collector . . . would not even raise his eyes to heaven, . . . 'O God, be merciful to me a sinner.' I tell you, the latter went home justified, not the former; for everyone who exalts himself will be humbled, and the one who humbles himself will be exalted."

Luke 18:10–14

First Hour

Listening God, when we're honest we have a clear picture of what needs to change. We trust that our Lenten prayer, fasting, and acts of charity can help us to be different. We pray for courage. Lord, hear our prayer.

Second Hour

Listening God, your heaven is filled with people we love who have died and now live with you. We sometimes ask them to pass our prayers on to you. Do we call that the Communion of Saints? We pray that you count us among your saints. Lord, hear our prayer.

Third Hour

Listening God, today's Scripture reminds us that some days we are more like the Pharisee than the tax collector. It matters to us that people pay attention. We pray that when people look at us, they notice more of you. Lord, hear our prayer.

Fourth Hour

Listening God, in the midst of our confusion, we sense your presence; we believe everything is possible with you and we know that you are God. Lord, hear our prayer.

Fifth Hour

Listening God, why do some people pray and still not receive what they long for? Unanswered prayer is a dilemma: we want to trust you for everything, but we don't understand when the answer is no. Help our unbelief. We pray for confidence. Lord, hear our prayer.

Sixth Hour

Listening God, some people walked through the doors of our school with heavy hearts this morning. May this community care for them and lift their spirits as we make our way through this day. Lord, hear our prayer.

Seventh Hour

Listening God, are we brave enough to follow the tax collector's example: to be quiet and take the last place instead of the first? Are we bold enough to witness to the Gospel and preach with our lives? We pray for courage. Lord, hear our prayer.

Eighth Hour

Listening God, we want to believe that the tax collector's example gave the Pharisee something to think about. We pray for eyes that pay attention so that we may be more aware of God's love tomorrow than we are today. Lord, hear our prayer.

Closing Blessing

We sign ourselves with the sign of our faith as we pray:
> **May God, Creator, bless us**
> **May God, Redeemer, heal us**
> **May the Holy Spirit enlighten us**
> **and give us all we need.**

TUESDAY

Fourth Week of Lent

Opening Prayer

We begin this class as we begin all things:
In the name of the Father
and of the Son
and of the Holy Spirit. Amen.

Scripture Reading

Jesus began to preach and say, "Repent, for the kingdom of heaven is at hand."

Matthew 4:17

First Hour

God of Covenant promises, there are people in our lives—at school, at home, at work—who have forgotten they are loved. We are sorry for every missed opportunity to let another human being know they matter. Forgive us, and prepare us for the Kingdom you promised.

Second Hour

God of Covenant promises, our history includes so many wasted days. This week will pass quickly, and there are days we have spent without making a difference, without choosing to live as someone who is a child of God. Forgive us, and prepare us for the Kingdom you promised.

Third Hour

God of Covenant promises, maybe part of the Lenten journey is that we will discover glimpses of this Kingdom already in our lives. We repent for not paying attention. Forgive us, and prepare us for the Kingdom you promised.

Fourth Hour

God of Covenant promises, we have been invited to live Lent by praying, fasting, and engaging in acts of charity and service. For the times we have failed to keep our Lenten promises, we ask your forgiveness. Forgive us, and prepare us for the Kingdom you promised.

Fifth Hour

God of Covenant promises, our Lenten promises included giving alms and performing acts of charity and service. We remember those who depend on our alms, who count on our sacrifice, in order to feed their children. We regret the times we have been unwilling to share what we have with those in need. Forgive us, and prepare us for the Kingdom you promised.

Sixth Hour

God of Covenant promises, we may have forgotten about those who cannot choose to abstain from food because they have no food. We are sorry for the times we have forgotten people for whom famine is a way of life. Forgive us, and prepare us for the Kingdom you promised.

Seventh Hour

God of Covenant promises, it is weeks since we marked our foreheads with ashes. What would Lent be like if the crosses on our foreheads were not smudged with ashes, but remained there until Easter? Would we be reminded of what we say we believe and who we say we are? Forgive us, and prepare us for the Kingdom you promised.

Eighth Hour

God of Covenant promises, we struggle with our identity as people who are destined for your Kingdom. We are not sure we are ready to become what we say we believe. Forgive us, and prepare us for the Kingdom you promised.

Closing Blessing

We sign ourselves with the sign of our faith as we pray:
> **May God, Creator, bless us**
> **May God, Redeemer, heal us**
> **May the Holy Spirit enlighten us**
> **and give us all we need.**

WEDNESDAY
Fourth Week of Lent

Opening Prayer

We begin this class as we begin all things:
**In the name of the Father
and of the Son
and of the Holy Spirit. Amen.**

Scripture Reading

*You have been told . . . what is good,
and what the LORD requires of you:
Only to do the right and to love goodness,
and to walk humbly with your God.*
Micah 6:8

First Hour

God of changed hearts, help us to seize this day and all the opportunities it brings for us to begin again. May we spend today doing what is right, and loving goodness.

Second Hour

God of changed hearts, do not let us be afraid of the surprises today will bring. Help us to be confident that you go into this day before us and beside us. May we spend today doing what is right, and loving goodness.

Third Hour

God of changed hearts, today we will do the best we can. Today we will assume that everyone else in this place is doing the best they can as well. May we spend today doing what is right, and loving goodness.

Fourth Hour

God of changed hearts, we are not always the first ones to reach out and lend a helping hand. Today let our hands be ready to help, let us liberate someone who feels isolated and alone and ignored. Today let us be changed. May we spend today doing what is right, and loving goodness.

Fifth Hour

God of changed hearts, let us be known as peacemakers. Let us empty our own lives and the life of our school of all violence: no aggressive words, no destructive actions, no caustic thoughts. We choose peace because this Lent we are discovering in a new way that we belong to you. May we spend today doing what is right, and loving goodness.

Sixth Hour

God of changed hearts, a lesson this Lent is that we can boldly tap into the power of prayer. Make us people of prayer. May we spend today doing what is right, and loving goodness.

Seventh Hour

God of changed hearts, it is a challenge to talk with someone outside my regular circle of friends. You are pretty clear about what is required of us: to be changed, to reach out and include the people who are on the outside. Stand with us as we spend a moment today inviting someone outside our circle to come in. May we spend today doing what is right, and loving goodness.

Eighth Hour

God of changed hearts, not all of us have been known as "bold" and "courageous." May this Lent lead us to accept the gift of daring when we are confronted with the opportunity to make a difference. May we spend today doing what is right, and loving goodness.

Closing Blessing

We sign ourselves with the sign of our faith as we pray:
> May God, Creator, bless us
> May God, Redeemer, heal us
> May the Holy Spirit enlighten us
> and give us all we need.

THURSDAY
Fourth Week of Lent

Opening Prayer

We begin this class as we begin all things:

**In the name of the Father
and of the Son
and of the Holy Spirit. Amen.**

Scripture Reading

*Yet even now, says the LORD,
return to me with your whole heart,
with fasting, and weeping, and mourning;
Rend your hearts, not your garments,
and return to the LORD, your God.
For gracious and merciful is he,
slow to anger, rich in kindness,
and relenting in punishment.*

Joel 2:12–13

First Hour

God who is love, it sounds like you expect every part of us to belong to you . . . to choose what is right. There may be parts of us we don't want to let go of. Habits—even bad habits—have a way of feeling essential to who we are. This Lent, give us confidence to return to you with our whole heart.

Second Hour

God who is love, we are confident that you envision not just us but the whole world returning to you. Perhaps as we each find our own way to peace, we will lead the world to peace . . . one child of God at a time. This Lent, give us confidence to return to you with our whole heart.

Third Hour

God who is love, if we let you into our hearts, we might see our families differently; the people who fill this school might not look the same. This Lent, give us confidence to return to you with our whole heart.

Fourth Hour

God who is love, for some of us our Lenten fast has included fasting from unkind words, gossip, or using your name as a curse. Your grace can make today's words different. This Lent, give us confidence to return to you with our whole heart.

Fifth Hour

God who is love, each and every one of us can take responsibility for being one voice for justice in a troubled world. Changed hearts make for changed voices. This Lent, give us confidence to return to you with our whole heart.

Sixth Hour

God who is love, there are people we love who struggle today with illnesses of mind, body, or spirit. We long to bless them with the strength and hope that all of us can find in the story of how you lived as a human being. This Lent, give us confidence to return to you with our whole heart.

Seventh Hour

God who is love, with changed hearts your earliest followers became bold proclaimers of the gospel. They had vision to believe in a Kingdom and courage to begin to build it. Can you do the same for us? This Lent, give us confidence to return to you with our whole heart.

Eighth Hour

God who is love, you say we need to change. You say that we choose to sin. You say that our poor choices ought to make us weep. This Lent, give us confidence to return to you with our whole heart.

Closing Blessing

We sign ourselves with the sign of our faith as we pray:
> **May God, Creator, bless us**
> **May God, Redeemer, heal us**
> **May the Holy Spirit enlighten us**
> **and give us all we need.**

FRIDAY

Fourth Week of Lent

Opening Prayer

We begin this class as we begin all things:
**In the name of the Father
and of the Son
and of the Holy Spirit. Amen.**

Scripture Reading

Then he handed him over to them to be crucified. So they took Jesus, and carrying the cross himself he went out to what is called the Place of the Skull, in Hebrew, Golgotha.
John 19:16–17

First Hour

God with us, they killed you. They gave you a cross to carry. When we have a big problem, people sometimes say we have a cross to carry. We call to mind the crosses we know in real life. By your holy cross, you redeemed the world.

Second Hour

God with us, they killed you. People gathered in the streets to stare at you. Sometimes we use people that way: we point them out, we make them the joke in our conversations. God, are you really in the people we use? By your holy cross, you redeemed the world.

Third Hour

God with us, they killed you. So many people joined you on your way. Your mom was there; she must have pushed through the crowd to get closer to you. By your holy cross, you redeemed the world.

Fourth Hour

God with us, they killed you. Artists have tried to imagine what your cross looked like—the weight, the roughness, the inevitability of it all. We know there are real crosses around us: depression . . . volatile family situations . . . friends who betray us. By your holy cross, you redeemed the world.

Fifth Hour

God with us, they killed you. Along the way the Roman soldiers decided you would never reach Calvary, so they pulled someone out of the crowd and you carried the cross together. Was he afraid to be so close to a man who was suffering? We also see suffering. Sometimes we look the other way when we could be carrying the cross together. By your holy cross, you redeemed the world.

Sixth Hour

God with us, they killed you. We don't let ourselves imagine your final steps: drag the cross . . . reach the top . . . drop the cross . . . lay your body flat against the wood . . . hammer smashes nails . . . splintered bone and splintered wood. We don't let ourselves imagine the truth: we have left hammer smashes and splintered spirits in someone's life. By your holy cross, you redeemed the world.

Seventh Hour

God with us, they killed you. Hanging on a cross, you say, "Forgive them." We do not always forgive so easily. We ask you to forgive us for the scenes in our lives that seemed like someone's road to Calvary. By your holy cross, you redeemed the world.

Eighth Hour

God with us, they killed you. We adore you, O Christ, and we bless you, because by your holy cross, you have redeemed the world.

Closing Blessing

We sign ourselves with the sign of our faith as we pray:
May God, Creator, bless us
May God, Redeemer, heal us
May the Holy Spirit enlighten us
and give us all we need.

FIFTH
WEEK OF LENT

MONDAY

Fifth Week of Lent

Opening Prayer

We begin this class as we begin all things:
**In the name of the Father
and of the Son
and of the Holy Spirit. Amen.**

Scripture Reading

"The words I have spoken to you are spirit and life."
John 6:63

First Hour

God living among us, your Word tells us that we have a unique role to play in the history of your people. May our prayer, fasting, and acts of charity help us to take our place in the salvation story. Help us to listen well and choose wisely. You are spirit and life.

Second Hour

God living among us, we call to mind our salvation story and we remember the men and women in history who have lost their lives in the struggle for peace. This Lent we hear your challenge to be people of peace. Help us to listen well and choose wisely. You are spirit and life.

Third Hour

God living among us, you say that when we fail we get the chance for new possibilities. Lent is a season for examining the bad and the good—for walking the road from crucifixion to resurrection. Help us to listen well and choose wisely. You are spirit and life.

Fourth Hour

God living among us, we have felt the spirit of your selfless love in parents and grandparents . . . in teachers and coaches . . . in brothers and sisters . . . in strangers who gave us a hand . . . in freshmen and seniors . . . in sophomores and juniors. Help us to listen well and choose wisely. You are spirit and life.

Fifth Hour

God living among us, we can feed someone's spirit by choosing words that feed their soul rather than starve it; we can quench the thirst of someone longing for just one kind word; we can take a minute to visit with a person who passes through our school unnoticed. Help us to listen well and choose wisely. You are spirit and life.

Sixth Hour

God living among us, we are grateful for the people in our lives and in our school who are willing to walk with us and help us unravel the mysteries of life and death and love and God. Help us to listen well and choose wisely. You are spirit and life.

Seventh Hour

God living among us, you continue to reveal your love for us through deeds and through words. Your love is a mystery we hope to understand at Lent's end. Help us to listen well and choose wisely. You are spirit and life.

Eighth Hour

God living among us, your word promises us eternal life. May this Lenten journey strengthen us in faith. Help us to listen well and choose wisely. You are spirit and life.

Closing Blessing

We sign ourselves with the sign of our faith as we pray:
>   **May God, Creator, bless us**
>   **May God, Redeemer, heal us**
>   **May the Holy Spirit enlighten us**
>   **and give us all we need.**

TUESDAY

Fifth Week of Lent

Opening Prayer

We begin this class as we begin all things:
**In the name of the Father
and of the Son
and of the Holy Spirit. Amen.**

Scripture Reading

*Do you call this a fast,
   a day acceptable to the LORD?
This, rather, is the fasting that I wish . . .
Setting free the oppressed,
   breaking every yoke;
Sharing your bread with the hungry,
   sheltering the oppressed and the homeless;
Clothing the naked when you see them,
   and not turning your back on your own.*
            Isaiah 58:5–7

First Hour

God, our hope, not everyone will be welcome at every lunch table. Some people are not a welcome addition when we get together after school, and our weekends have a very select guest list. Maybe we'll need to make some changes before this day is acceptable to you.

Second Hour

God, our hope, on this Lenten day, we will ask ourselves what separates us from one another. Maybe we'll need to make some changes before this day is acceptable to you.

Third Hour

God, our hope, we think there may be habits or ways of thinking that we hold on to so tightly that they build walls. What would happen if we tore down the walls we build when we don't tell the truth? Maybe we'll need to make some changes before this day is acceptable to you.

Fourth Hour

God, our hope, what would happen if we fasted from the habit of taking everything personally? What if we fasted from suffering because of what we imagine someone thinks of us and decided to be happy with the fact that you think we are enough? Maybe we'll need to make some changes before this day is acceptable to you.

Fifth Hour

God, our hope, we could fast from the habit of making assumptions. We could find the courage to ask questions and express what we really need. Maybe we'll need to make some changes before this day is acceptable to you.

Sixth Hour

God, our hope, what if we fasted from the habit of not using the talents we received from you? We could choose to simply do our best—not to be perfect, but to be whole. Maybe we'll need to make some changes before this day is acceptable to you.

Seventh Hour

God, our hope, this Lent we get to choose to set the oppressed free, to share our bread, to provide a shelter for the homeless, to not turn our backs. Maybe we'll need to make some changes before this day is acceptable to you.

Eighth Hour

God, our hope, you love us enough to let us choose. You do not assume we want you in our lives, but you patiently wait for us to choose to follow. Maybe we'll need to make some changes before this day is acceptable to you.

Closing Blessing

We sign ourselves with the sign of our faith as we pray:

> **May God, Creator, bless us**
> **May God, Redeemer, heal us**
> **May the Holy Spirit enlighten us**
> **and give us all we need.**

WEDNESDAY

Fifth Week of Lent

Opening Prayer

We begin this class as we begin all things:
**In the name of the Father
and of the Son
and of the Holy Spirit. Amen.**

Scripture Reading

"If one of your kinsmen in any community is in need in the land which the LORD, your God, is giving you, you shall not harden your heart nor close your hand to him in his need."

Deuteronomy 15:7

First Hour

Generous One, we pause this morning to ask ourselves if we live in a way that makes it obvious that the love of God is at work here. Like all who love you, we will not harden our hearts.

Second Hour

Generous One, we are grateful for the people who provide us with what we need to keep going during difficult times. Like all who love you, we will not harden our hearts.

Third Hour

Generous One, it is important that we are honest about what we really need and what is extra. Today we ponder the confusing truth: it is your job to generously provide all that the world needs and it is our job to spread it around so everyone has enough. Like all who love you, we will not harden our hearts.

Fourth Hour

Generous One, as we explore the universe beyond our planet, we wonder who is paying attention to protecting and sustaining your generosity. This Lent can be the beginning of a gentler universe. Like all who love you, we will not harden our hearts.

Fifth Hour

Generous One, our school is filled with teachers, staff, coaches, nurses, cafeteria workers, and custodians who seem to sense when we need attention. May we become aware of the adults who know how hard we work and keep telling us that all things are possible. Like all who love you, we will not harden our hearts.

Sixth Hour

Generous One, the rhythm of Lent offers us a way to discover the truth—even if it is difficult and makes us uncomfortable. Like all who love you, we will not harden our hearts.

Seventh Hour

Generous One, we see people in our school who always try to do their best, people who don't ignore the opportunity to speak in defense of someone who is weak, people who are your eyes noticing every bit of goodness here. Each of us must grapple with an essential life question now: Am I that person? Like all who love you, we will not harden our hearts.

Eighth Hour

Generous One, this Lent is not the first time you have invited us to come away and spend some time with you. The days of Lent are nearly over. We continue to pray . . . to fast . . . to share what we have with someone in need. Like all who love you, we will not harden our hearts.

Closing Blessing

We sign ourselves with the sign of our faith as we pray:
   May God, Creator, bless us
   May God, Redeemer, heal us
   May the Holy Spirit enlighten us
   and give us all we need.

THURSDAY
Fifth Week of Lent

Opening Prayer

We begin this class as we begin all things:
**In the name of the Father
and of the Son
and of the Holy Spirit. Amen.**

Scripture Reading

*A clean heart create for me, God;
   renew in me a steadfast spirit.
Do not drive me from your presence,
   nor take from me your holy spirit.
Restore my joy in your salvation;
   sustain in me a willing spirit.*
                    Psalm 51:12–14

First Hour

Steadfast God, we need to be renewed in these Lenten days, and we are realizing that part of becoming new is asking for your forgiveness. We pray for a spirit of mercy, so we may be able to forgive a person we love who has hurt us. We ask because we believe there is joy in your salvation.

Second Hour

Steadfast God, may we be strengthened to stand up for what we know is right and true and holy—even when we know there will be consequences for our actions. We ask because we believe there is joy in your salvation.

Third Hour

Steadfast God, some of us can remember times when our words and actions denied any attachment to you. Do not ever take your holy spirit from us. We ask because we believe there is joy in your salvation.

Fourth Hour

Steadfast God, you are with us even when we alienate people who are an essential part of our lives. For the times we have separated ourselves from our parents and stepparents by speaking about them unkindly or with sarcasm or implying that we would rather belong to someone else, we ask your forgiveness. We ask because we believe there is joy in your salvation.

Fifth Hour

Steadfast God, for the times we have repeated secrets, betrayed confidences, or denied that we are really friends, we ask your forgiveness. Help us to ask the forgiveness of our friends as well. We ask because we believe there is joy in your salvation.

Sixth Hour

Steadfast God, many of us here right now have brothers and sisters. For the times we have isolated ourselves and refused to share our hopes and dreams and lives with them, we ask your forgiveness. We ask because we believe there is joy in your salvation.

Seventh Hour

Steadfast God, there are those who feel like they have been driven from your presence . . . crippled by anxiety . . . frozen with fear about deciding . . . blind to any glimpse of you . . . drained of feeling. Renew their willing spirits. We ask because we believe there is joy in your salvation.

Eighth Hour

Steadfast God, we ask for the gift of boldness—that the practices of this Lent make us bold enough to turn away from anything that is not you. We ask because we believe there is joy in your salvation.

Closing Blessing

We sign ourselves with the sign of our faith as we pray:
> **May God, Creator, bless us**
> **May God, Redeemer, heal us**
> **May the Holy Spirit enlighten us**
> **and give us all we need.**

FRIDAY

Fifth Week of Lent

Opening Prayer

We begin this class as we begin all things:
**In the name of the Father
and of the Son
and of the Holy Spirit. Amen.**

Scripture Reading

*He advanced a little and fell to the ground and prayed
that if it were possible the hour might pass by him; he said,
"Abba, Father, all things are possible to you. Take this cup
away from me, but not what I will but what you will."*

Mark 14:35–36

First Hour

Living God, all things are possible with you. We pray that we will
not take for granted our opportunities to make a difference in the
world. Not our will, but your will.

Second Hour

Living God, all things are possible with you. We pray that we
will not miss the gifts this community has to offer by isolating
ourselves and trying to make it on our own. Help us to see that the
best way to travel is together. Not our will, but your will.

Third Hour

Living God, all things are possible with you. We ask that we will
give long and serious thought to breaking ranks with a culture that
judges our achievement by the number of activities we are involved
in. We have learned that you use a different measure. Not our will,
but your will.

Fourth Hour

Living God, all things are possible with you. We were worried that you would lead us to places we didn't want to go. Remembering the times we deliberately chose to turn and walk the other way, we pray that our choice of whether or not to follow will be different the next time you point the way. Not our will, but your will.

Fifth Hour

Living God, all things are possible with you. There are countless people—religious sisters, nursing home aides, and foster parents—who dedicate their lives to serving others who are in need. Is that what you are calling us to do? Not our will, but your will.

Sixth Hour

Living God, all things are possible with you. Lent reminds us that sometimes life is a challenge. May today's struggles remind us that human beings were made to depend on God and on one another. Not our will, but your will.

Seventh Hour

Living God, all things are possible with you. We want to dare to tell the truth. Fill us with the grace we need to speak when it is our turn, to stand up for what is right, and to shine light on our illusions so that we can see the world and you more clearly. Not our will, but your will.

Eighth Hour

Living God, all things are possible with you. When we finally stop for the day—after school, after practice, after our job, after homework, and as we close our eyes to sleep tonight—let us take a moment to consider this Lent. We are moving into the holiest of weeks. We want to remember that you love us. Not our will, but your will.

Closing Blessing

We sign ourselves with the sign of our faith as we pray:
> May God, Creator, bless us
> May God, Redeemer, heal us
> May the Holy Spirit enlighten us
> and give us all we need.

SIXTH
WEEK OF LENT

MONDAY

Sixth Week of Lent

Opening Prayer

We begin this class as we begin all things:
**In the name of the Father
and of the Son
and of the Holy Spirit. Amen.**

Scripture Reading

*For this is our God,
    whose people we are,
    God's well-tended flock.
Oh, that today you would hear his voice.*
                        Psalm 95:7

First Hour

God of ordinary people, we want to hear your voice. May we welcome your voice in the person of the migrant farm worker whose labor brings us our food. "This is our God, whose people we are."

Second Hour

God of ordinary people, we want to hear your voice. May we welcome your voice in the language of refugees; alone in our communities, they move with courage and in hope. "This is our God, whose people we are."

Third Hour

God of ordinary people, we want to hear your voice. May we welcome your voice in the immigrant artist . . . athlete . . . doctor, who are part of your flock. They bring the gifts you gave them, the gifts that we receive. "This is our God, whose people we are."

Fourth Hour

God of ordinary people, we want to hear your voice. Are there prophets among us—members of our community who use words like justice, equality, and everyone? We do not always welcome the voices of prophets because they make us uncomfortable with the way things are now and the way things could be. "This is our God, whose people we are."

Fifth Hour

God of ordinary people, we want to hear your voice. You call us your "flock." A flock of sheep can be a difficult group to keep together: they like to wander, they explore in their own sweet time, and they have minds of their own. But sheep know the sound of the shepherd's voice . . . and they turn toward the shepherd when they hear it. "This is our God, whose people we are."

Sixth Hour

God of ordinary days, this is the week you walk to your Calvary. We can only hope that our Lenten prayer and sacrifice has made us ready to march into the world—into our families, our schools, our jobs, our friendships—in order to carry out your will. "This is our God, whose people we are."

Seventh Hour

God of ordinary days, is it both peace and restlessness that we wish for? May our observance of these Lenten days prepare us to be turned, disturbed, and stirred by visions of unknown things and new ideas that can shape the world we know into the Kingdom you offer. "This is our God, whose people we are."

Eighth Hour

God of ordinary days, our Lenten school days are nearly over. Help us to carry our Lenten practice into the ordinary days. May we be people who pray, who fast, and who serve each other. "This is our God, whose people we are."

Closing Blessing

We sign ourselves with the sign of our faith as we pray:

> **May God, Creator, bless us**
> **May God, Redeemer, heal us**
> **May the Holy Spirit enlighten us**
> **and give us all we need.**

TUESDAY

Sixth Week of Lent

Opening Prayer

We begin this class as we begin all things:
**In the name of the Father
and of the Son
and of the Holy Spirit. Amen.**

Scripture Reading

*He went out and saw a tax collector named Levi sitting at
the customs post. He said to him, "Follow me." And leaving
everything behind, he got up and followed him. . . . "Why do
you eat with tax collectors and sinners?" Jesus said. . . . "I
have not come to call the righteous to repentance but sinners."*
Luke 5:27–32

First Hour

God of invitations, we are learning to expect to hear your voice . . .
and little by little you can expect to hear our voices echo yours.
May our observance of Lent make a difference as the sounds of a
living Kingdom of God are heard loud and clear. You still invite us
to follow you.

Second Hour

God of invitations, you invited us into Lent, and our prayer,
fasting, and service reminds us that we are called to build your
Kingdom. We pray that you will fill us with a spirit of wisdom to
know how to make a difference and a spirit of courage to say yes.
You still invite us to follow you.

Third Hour

God of invitations, we accepted your Lenten invitation and
responded with prayer, fasting, and acts of charity. We still have
questions, and so we pray that we will listen carefully to your voice
within our hearts and to your prophetic voice in others. You still
invite us to follow you.

Fourth Hour

God of invitations, soon it will be time for you to surrender: the cup will not pass and the cross will be waiting. This Lent, help us to surrender ourselves to the holy plan you have for our lives. You still invite us to follow you.

Fifth Hour

God of invitations, you invited a tax collector, fishermen, women, lepers, and people who were blind, and their individual yeses made a difference. They remind us that there is a place at the table for ordinary people like us. You still invite us to follow you.

Sixth Hour

God of invitations, we now realize that you are not breaking into our lives from the outside, but that you are breaking into life, into the real world, from inside each of us . . . if we say yes. You still invite us to follow you.

Seventh Hour

God of invitations, this Lent may have given some of us a new way of seeing the people who share our lives. The people we love . . . care for . . . argue with . . . make up with . . . all have the potential of giving us a glimpse of who you are. You still invite us to follow you.

Eighth Hour

God of invitations, this Lent may have given us a new way of listening. We pray that we are more able to tell the difference between a partial truth that is easy to hear and the whole truth that challenges us to do things differently. You still invite us to follow you.

Closing Blessing

We sign ourselves with the sign of our faith as we pray:
> **May God, Creator, bless us**
> **May God, Redeemer, heal us**
> **May the Holy Spirit enlighten us**
> **and give us all we need.**

WEDNESDAY

Sixth Week of Lent

Opening Prayer

We begin this class as we begin all things:
In the name of the Father
and of the Son
and of the Holy Spirit. Amen.

Scripture Reading

"Take care not to perform righteous deeds in order that people may see them. . . . When you give alms, do not blow a trumpet before you . . . to win the praise of others. . . . But when you give alms, do not let your left hand know what your right is doing, so that your almsgiving may be secret."

Matthew 6:1–4

First Hour

Giver of all good gifts, we bring our alms and offer the gift of truth in our lives. May this Lent empower us to say what we mean with kindness and candor.

Second Hour

Giver of all good gifts, we bring our alms and offer the gift of mystery in our lives. May this Lent empower us to embrace the questions that lead us to the truth.

Third Hour

Giver of all good gifts, we bring our alms and offer the gift of time in our lives. May this Lent empower us to honor time at the beginning of every day to remind us of who we are—and to whom we belong.

Fourth Hour

Giver of all good gifts, we bring our alms and offer the gift of forgiveness. May this Lent empower us to stand in the shower of your mercy with the person we find it hardest to forgive.

Fifth Hour

Giver of all good gifts, we bring our alms and offer the gift of patience. May this Lent empower us to be gentle with all that is unfinished in our lives.

Sixth Hour

Giver of all good gifts, we bring our alms and offer the gift of service. May this Lent empower us to make a difference in the life of someone who is faced with circumstances they never imagined were possible.

Seventh Hour

Giver of all good gifts, we bring our alms and offer the gift of open arms. May this Lent empower us to have the courage to release the people we love into God's hands.

Eighth Hour

Giver of all good gifts, we bring our alms and offer the gift of risk taking. May this Lent empower us to face our fears and take action . . . to seek justice even though we have to pay a price for our action.

Closing Blessing

We sign ourselves with the sign of our faith as we pray:
> **May God, Creator, bless us**
> **May God, Redeemer, heal us**
> **May the Holy Spirit enlighten us**
> **and give us all we need.**

HOLY THURSDAY

Opening Prayer

We begin this class as we begin all things:
**In the name of the Father
and of the Son
and of the Holy Spirit. Amen.**

Scripture Reading

So when he had washed their feet [and] put his garments back on and reclined at table again, he said to them, "Do you realize what I have done for you? . . . If I, therefore, the master and teacher, have washed your feet, you ought to wash one another's feet."

John 13:12–14

First Hour

Humble Servant, as you kneel with a towel in your hands and a bowl of water at your side, you teach us that there is more than one way to make you really present in our school. Do we realize what you have done for us?

Second Hour

Humble Servant, you gathered your followers for the Passover meal and turned everything they thought about you upside down. The questions about who you are and what that means overwhelm us sometimes. Do we realize what you have done for us?

Third Hour

Humble Servant, if we follow you, we must be ready to "wash the feet of others." It didn't make sense to your Apostles and it doesn't always make sense to us—that's not the way the world works. Do we realize what you have done for us?

Fourth Hour

Humble Servant, we struggle to learn the Last Supper lesson: to look at the people around us and pick up a towel . . . or pick up a book that drops in the hall . . . or pick up the reputation of someone who has been wounded by words. You want us to look straight ahead and see you. Do we realize what you have done for us?

Fifth Hour

Humble Servant, sometimes we are the person who needs to have someone else "wash our feet." Accepting help can be hard, but false pride is not what you ask us to bring into our schools, our families, our friendships, or our world. You ask us for humility. Do we realize what you have done for us?

Sixth Hour

Humble Servant, you came to serve and not to be served, help us to understand that if we love and serve you we must love and serve everyone. You served everyone—whether it looked like they deserved it or not. Do we realize what you have done for us?

Seventh Hour

Humble Servant, you gathered with your friends for a meal and washed their feet. If we are paying attention to you and your friends, it looks like the service and the meal go together. Is that what you dream for your Church? for your followers? for us? Do we realize what you have done for us?

Eighth Hour

Humble Servant, you promise to take care of whatever we need—even if that means filling a basin with water, tying a towel around your waist, kneeling down, and washing our feet. Do we realize what you have done for us?

Closing Blessing

We sign ourselves with the sign of our faith as we pray:
>May God, Creator, bless us
>May God, Redeemer, heal us
>May the Holy Spirit enlighten us
>and give us all we need.

GOOD FRIDAY

Opening Prayer

We begin this class as we begin all things:
**In the name of the Father
and of the Son
and of the Holy Spirit. Amen.**

Scripture Reading

*He humbled himself,
becoming obedient to death,
even death on a cross.
Because of this, God greatly exalted him
and bestowed on him the name
that is above every name . . .
Jesus Christ is Lord.*

Philippians 2:8–11

First Hour

God among us, they thought you were a criminal! Wasn't there another way? As our Lenten journey ends, may we know that Jesus Christ is Lord.

Second Hour

God among us, you obeyed because you trusted in the plan of salvation. We want to trust your plan for our lives. As our Lenten journey ends, may we know that Jesus Christ is Lord.

Third Hour

God among us, we fight back in so many ways: we gossip, we ignore someone who cares about us, we pout or shout or threaten. You were a human being too, but you didn't do any of those things—you humbled yourself and obeyed. As our Lenten journey ends, may we know that Jesus Christ is Lord.

Fourth Hour

God among us, we are not always sure what it means to obey. Help us to see that you are at work in our lives—right here among us. As our Lenten journey ends, may we know that Jesus Christ is Lord.

Fifth Hour

God among us, soldiers arrested you, whipped you, stripped you of everything, and brought you to the cross. There are people in our lives who have hurt us, and we call them to mind and pray for them right now [pause]. As our Lenten journey ends, may we know that Jesus Christ is Lord.

Sixth Hour

God among us, there must have been a moment when your human nature wondered if you had anything left to give. We have had those moments—when school is just too much or when life at home is a challenge or when it feels like we haven't a friend in the world. As our Lenten journey ends, may we know that Jesus Christ is Lord.

Seventh Hour

God among us, the cross must have been a lonely place. When our lives seem like dark and lonely places, remind us of your Good Friday. As our Lenten journey ends, may we know that Jesus Christ is Lord.

Eighth Hour

God among us, there was a moment—after the insults and the mocking, after the beating and the pain, after the abandonment and the cross—when you knew it was finished. It was finished, and because you are God, everything became possible and we can live forever in the Kingdom. As our Lenten journey ends, may we know that Jesus Christ is Lord.

Closing Blessing

We sign ourselves with the sign of our faith as we pray:

May God, Creator, bless us
May God, Redeemer, heal us
May the Holy Spirit enlighten us
and give us all we need.